MW00978791

TAMING AND TRAINING COCKATOOS
KW-071

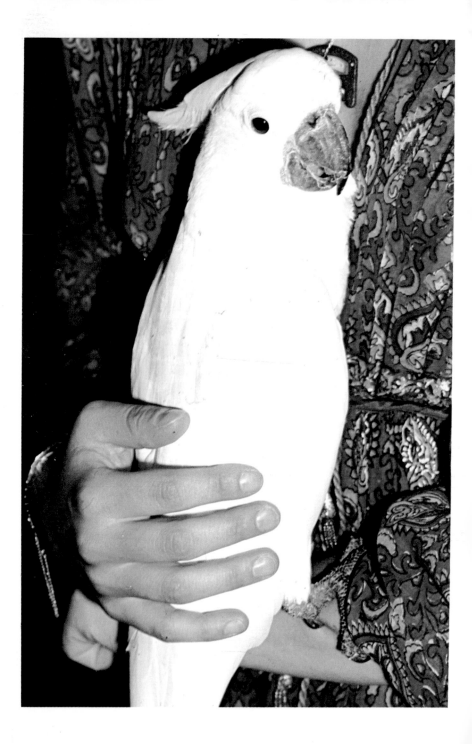

CONTENTS

Photography: Dr. Gerald Allen, Dr. Herbert R. Axelrod, Isabelle Francais, Earl Grossman, Manolo Guevara, Ray Hanson, Ralph Kaehler, S. Kates, P. Leysen, A.J. Mobbs, Horst Müller, Fritz Prenzel, L. Robinson, San Diego Zoo, Ken Stepnell, Vogelpark Walsrode.

Overleaf: One of the greatest delights in owning a cockatoo is the trust that is established between bird and owner. *Title page:* Cockatoos are different from one another in temperament. Some are timid and unresponsive, whereas others are bold and demonstrative.

© **1988 by T.F.H. Publications, Inc.**

Distributed in the UNITED STATES by T.F.H. Publications, Inc., One T.F.H. Plaza, Neptune City, NJ 07753; in CANADA to the Pet Trade by H & L Pet Supplies Inc., 27 Kingston Crescent, Kitchener, Ontario N2B 2T6; Rolf C. Hagen Ltd., 3225 Sartelon Street, Montreal 382 Quebec; in CANADA to the Book Trade by Macmillan of Canada (A Division of Canada Publishing Corporation), 164 Commander Boulevard, Agincourt, Ontario M1S 3C7; in ENGLAND by T.F.H. Publications Limited, Cliveden House/Priors Way/Bray, Maidenhead, Berkshire SL6 2HP, England; in AUSTRALIA AND THE SOUTH PACIFIC by T.F.H. (Australia) Pty. Ltd., Box 149, Brookvale 2100 N.S.W., Australia; in NEW ZEALAND by Ross Haines & Son, Ltd., 18 Monmouth Street, Grey Lynn, Auckland 2, New Zealand; in SINGAPORE AND MALAYSIA by MPH Distributors (S) Pte., Ltd., 601 Sims Drive, #03/07/21, Singapore 1438; in the PHILIPPINES by Bio-Research, 5 Lippay Street, San Lorenzo Village, Makati Rizal; in SOUTH AFRICA by Multipet Pty. Ltd., 30 Turners Avenue, Durban 4001. Published by T.F.H. Publications, Inc. Manufactured in the United States of America by T.F.H. Publications, Inc.

TAMING AND TRAINING COCKATOOS

RISA TEITLER

Cockatoos respond well to affection and have a potential for making good pets for some people. They must be cared for properly, of course, and must be given a sensible taming and training regimen in order for their owners to get the most from them in terms of enjoyment. **Above:** The author and one of her trained cockatoos, which is demonstrating how well it responds to affection. **Facing page:** Using a natural wooden perch as a step in the taming/training process.

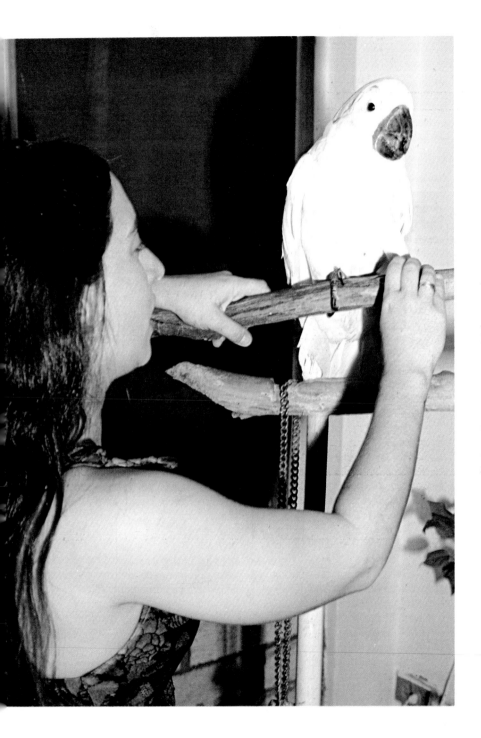

Introduction

Cockatoos are perhaps the most interesting, comical birds with which I have ever come in contact. Their outstanding intelligence and emotional makeup have made them my favorite birds of all the many species of parrots. However, cockatoos are not the best pets for most people; these birds require a great deal of attention, need a great deal of room and make a great deal of noise.

When handled properly, a cockatoo can become an affectionate pet, but if handled improperly it can become a dangerous menace. Don't buy a cockatoo unless you have had ample experience with smaller parrots, have been successful in taming them and have learned about their training and dietary requirements.

In residential neighborhoods a cockatoo can be a public nuisance, for it will insist upon heralding the sunrise no matter what the hour. Your pet may become so attached to you that it will scream all day until you get home from work, or it may pull out its feathers in protest at being left alone.

Be aware of all the drawbacks of owning a cockatoo and if you are still interested, read the following pages carefully; they were written to assist you in socializing and successfully handling a newly acquired wild cockatoo.

A separate chapter on illness has been intentionally avoided, for it is hoped that the cockatoo owner will seek out an expert in avian medicine whenever ill health is suspected.

COCKATOOS IN GENERAL

All cockatoos belong to the family Cacatuidae and inhabit Australia and some of the islands of the South Pacific. Some species of cockatoos range as far north as the Philippines. The members of the family Cacatuidae vary tremendously in size and appearance, from the small, familiar cockatiel to the large, rare palm cockatoo.

Most people think of cockatoos as white birds with yellow crests, but there are also black cockatoos. These black cockatoos are rare and expensive, and most specimens are kept as exhibits in wildlife parks, zoos or other public attractions.

The most common pet cockatoos (besides the cockatiel) are the sulphur-crested and salmon-crested. The umbrella or white-crested cockatoo is beginning to win popularity as a pet because of its relatively low price and its gentle nature. Goffin's cockatoo has recently become more available because of the destruction of its natural

Facing page: The cheek patches of the palm cockatoo turn dark red when the bird is in an excited state.

8

The identification of the various species and subspecies of cockatoos will be easier once you become familiar with the way subtleties of coloration, as well as such basic considerations as where the bird comes from, size and relative configuration of anatomical structures like the beak and tail affect identification. The photos on this page and the facing page represent three different species within the genus Cacatua.

habitat in Indonesia, due to development for commercial interests.

The red-vented cockatoo, native to the Philippines, is also seasonally available, mostly because of its propensity for

Cockatoo species vary widely in price, but even the least expensive of them should be introduced only to homes in which they'll be given good care.

destroying cultivated fields. All cockatoos are fond of feeding on farmland crops, especially corn. For this reason the Australian government has an open hunting season on its native cockatoo species, but it is stubborn in refusing to export them for the pet trade. The future may show this to be a wise attitude, for the Australian birds may be the only species to escape devastation due to the high monetary value of the birds in the pet trade.

All cockatoos have strong bills that are made of hardened keratin and colored either beige or black, depending on the species. The feet of most cockatoos are black. All have a conspicuous periophthalmic ring, which may be white, blue or purple (as in the bare-eyed corella). The white cockatoos show little sexual dimorphism, except for eye color; in mature males the iris is black or dark brown and in females the iris may be red or red-brown. Immature birds often are mistaken for females, for the iris is usually light brown. The black cockatoos such as the gang-gang and red-tailed have noticeable differences in plumage according to sex, but the palms and yellow-tailed cockatoos do not. It matters little what sex your cockatoo is if you have bought it for a pet, but for those who desire to attempt a breeding experiment, considerable care must be taken to be sure that birds of the opposite sex are acquired.

All cockatoos have a bald spot on the cranium, covered by the crest feathers, and all have powder down beneath the outer layer of plumage. The powder

Cockatoos vary in personality from bird to bird. Pictured is a sulphur-crested cock-atoo flanked by Major Mitchell's, or Leadbeater's, cockatoos.

down provides insulation to keep the body temperature constant, but more remarkably this down sheds a thick powder which is used for waterproofing and cleaning the outer feathers. Although many varieties of game birds have powder down, cockatoos are the only parrots that have powder down feathers.

When you rub your hands on the feathers of a healthy bird, you usually find your hand coated with the powder!

All cockatoos, except for the cockatiel, have short bobbed tails. Some have an erectile crest which dips upward even when the bird is in a relaxed state; others have a recumbent crest that lies flat on

Facing page: A salmon-crested cockatoo. *Right:* A red-vented cockatoo. *Below:* Sulphur-crested cockatoos "conversing."

the head unless the bird raises it in excitement or when alighting after flight.

Most cockatoos are sedate creatures with calm dispositions, but some individuals may be extremely nervous. Most are gentle, but aggressive cockatoos are not uncommon.

The life expectancy of cockatoos, like other large parrots, is lengthy, from 30 to 50 years. Some cockatoos, especially the greater sulphur-crested cockatoo from Australia, have survived in captivity for 60 to 70 years.

When fed and housed properly, cockatoos are generally hardy birds, but, like people, some will catch any bug that is in the air. These individuals must obviously be given extra shelter from the elements and fed an enriched diet at all times.

Because of their long life expectancy, a five to ten-year-old bird is not too old for taming and training. Undoubtedly, the younger the bird the more easily it is tamed, but do not shy away from an older bird if it appears to be a steady individual.

Most cockatoos are very intelligent, adaptable creatures; unfortunately, some are so nervous that their intelligence is difficult to perceive. Their life cycles are similar to the human life cycle: infancy, childhood, adolescence, young adulthood, middle age and old age. Although there is considerable controversy concerning the minimum reproductive age of cockatoos, they are reproductively mature at about eight years of age and will continue to reproduce into their twenties and thirties.

In captivity, the urge to reproduce is affected by many factors, but there is not enough space to discuss these variables in this volume. In short, you cannot expect any male and female cockatoo pair successfully to rear young or even lay eggs even though all environmental circumstances seem correct. Cockatoos must like one another in order to breed, but it would take a separate book to fully detail the relationship that breeding birds can achieve.

Cockatoos are not reputed to be good talking birds, but given the right training a cockatoo can become an excellent talker. The voice quality is high-pitched and does not rival the human tone of the Amazon parrots, but with consistent training a cockatoo can master many different words and sounds.

A large flock of cockatoos leaving a large tree; photographed in Australia. Many species are still abundant in their range, but this should not be an excuse for indiscriminate hunting and collecting.

Left: *The sulphur-crested cockatoo has a comparatively large crest, but others, such as Goffin's cockatoo, have smaller crests.* **Below and facing page:** *Not every cockatoo will allow its owner to take such liberties in handling.*

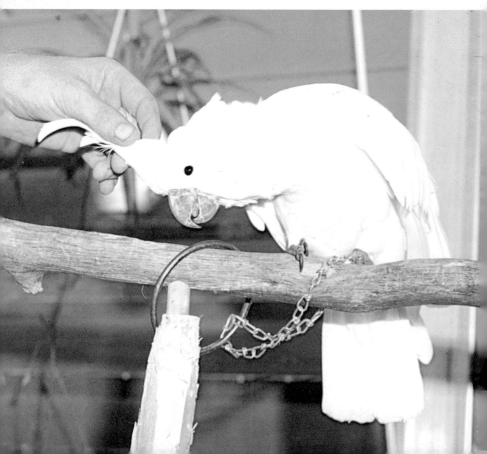

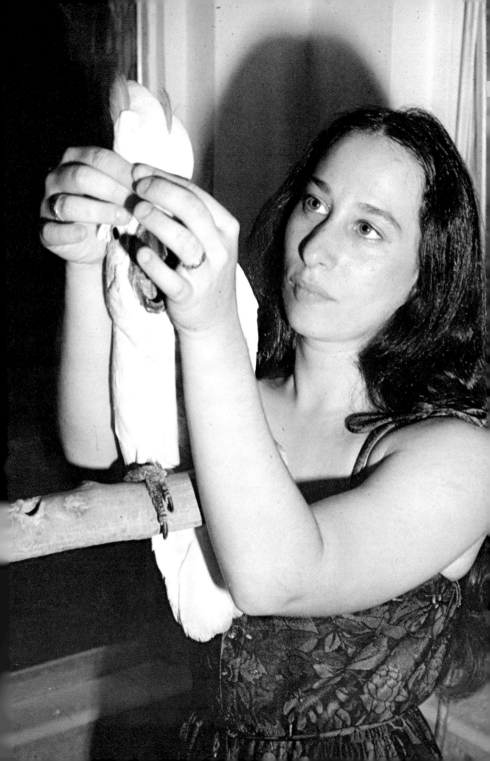

Cockatoo Species

The most common cockatoos in captivity are the sulphur- crested varieties. These include the greater sulphur from Australia and the triton, often called the blue-eyed cockatoo (the triton and blue-eyed are actually different). The dwarf sulphur is a tiny cockatoo, about eight inches in total length, while the greater sulphur is over eighteen inches from head to tail.

There are subspecies of both the greater sulphur and triton which have become more and more common in captivity since the wholesale market has found it profitable to sell them commercially. The average buyer does not really know the difference between the true Australian greater and a sub-species from a nearby island and often does not care. The potential of these subspecies to become tame pets is as good as that of the Australian varieties, but the buyer should educate himself to differentiate between them to avoid misunderstandings with the retailer.

The white-crested or umbrella cockatoo is very similar to the salmon-crested or Moluccan cockatoo and is probably a close relative. Both varieties vary greatly in size, and this probably represents subspecies of both kinds of birds. Size is incidental for pet potential, but if you are buying birds for breeding, buy the largest and most beautifully proportioned specimens that you can find.

Leadbeater's, or Major Mitchell's, cockatoo is unbelievably beautiful and quite rare in captivity. These birds are native to the interior of the Australian continent and are very difficult to obtain outside of Australia. The basic plumage is rose colored on the breast, abdomen and face. The crest is deep rose with either a white or yellow band crossing the center of the feathers; the tips of the crest feathers are white. The yellow or white band in the crest once again probably denotes two separate subspecies, but if you are lucky enough to acquire a Leadbeater's, do not be choosy about the color of the banding in the crest!

A more common cockatoo in captivity is the citron-crested cockatoo. A fairly small bird, the citron-crested cockatoo is very similar to the sulphur-crested, but the crest is a deep orange and orange feathers appear over the ears.

Cockatoos having a short, recumbent, inconspicuous crest include the corella, Goffin's, the red-vented, and Ducorp's. These are small birds and when they are available, they are usually inexpensive compared to their flamboyantly crested cousins.

Facing page: A red-tailed cockatoo. These birds are not commonly kept in captivity.

Left: *Little corella.* **Below:** *A pair of palm cockatoos.* **Facing page:** *Galah, also called rose-breasted cockatoo.*

The inexpensive little corella is a fantastic talker, with an excellent voice quality. Due to their smaller size they are often more easily housed in captivity and can be very satisfying, affectionate pets.

The galah or rose-breasted cockatoo is a beautiful but expensive bird in the United States. A fairly small bird, it is rarely seen for sale in the States and is regarded by most as an aviary bird. In its native Australia, the galah is abundant and very inexpensive. In that country it is a common house pet, and in fact the Australians with whom I have spoken regarded the galah as an excellent house pet.

The species of black cockatoos—the palms, red-tailed, yellow-tailed, white-tailed, glossy and gang-gang—are very rare in captivity. I have never heard one speak, but I believe that the potential for speech is there. These are high-strung, docile birds, generally speaking, and are most often kept as aviary birds. I have observed that these black cockatoos seem to have unusual dietary requirements; before obtaining such a bird, the potential owner should be certain to study the available information regarding its habits.

The cockatiel should be mentioned here, for it is a member of the subfamily of cockatoos. This is the only bird in this group that has a long tapering tail and is very common as a house pet throughout the world. A separate volume entitled *TAMING AND TRAINING COCKATIELS* details all facets of obtaining, taming and maintaining a cockatiel in captivity and it is readily available in most pet and bird shops.

Note the difference in size between the smaller Timor cockatoo and the obviously larger greater sulphur-crested cockatoo.

The rose-breasted cockatoo perched on top of the cage is allowed freedom of the room while the sulphur-crested cockatoo is restricted to its cage because of the damage it does to the room with its beak when allowed freedom.

Only a tame cockatoo will let a hand reach out to touch it as shown in the photos at left and below. **Facing page:** These birds, well trained and accustomed to being handled, pose fearlessly with their trainer.

Personality

Cockatoos are highly sophisticated, individualistic creatures, and there is great diversity in personality from bird to bird. Once domesticated, they emotionally resemble young children. They have an inexhaustible craving for attention and will go to any length to gain it. With good training, the majority of cockatoos will become affectionate birds which adore your caress. They look forward to being handled, kissed and hugged close to your body.

This is not the rule, however, and some birds may never relax completely and enjoy being petted. Some are so nervous that they show alarm by fluffing up the feathers and raising the crest whenever you approach. Even these birds can usually be convinced that petting is nice and worthwhile, but with very frightened individuals it may take a long time.

Most cockatoos always want to be the center of attention, and if you are entertaining guests or have other pet parrots, the cockatoo will prance up and down on its perch or in its cage, whistle, scream, or do whatever it takes to become the center of attention. They are not able to set their own interests aside for the welfare or benefit of others. This is not meant to be considered a flaw in the personality, for unlike children who grow out of the "Give me" stage, cockatoos do not. Throughout life

Below: A greater sulphur-crested letting off some steam. Note that the feathers of one wing are clipped.
***Facing page:** Gang-gang cockatoo.*

Cockatoos vary in their individual temperaments and talents. Some are easily trained to perch on the hand (left), while others take a long time to adapt to even their first lessons in stick training (right). But most cockatoos want to be the center of attention, and, like the bird in the photo below, will put on some kind of show to get it.

they are self-centered, egocentric birds. For this reason, cockatoos are not recommended as safe pets for young children. If kept in a household with very young children, care must be taken to be certain that neither suffers damage at the hands of the other.

Cockatoos are very attractive, and children often do not realize the dangerous potential of their bite. Always supervise interaction between your pet cockatoo and your child. Never let the child handle the bird unattended, no matter how gentle the parrot may

Mutual preening is part of the courtship of sulphur-crested cockatoos.

This photo illustrates the delicate coloration of the galah, or rose-breasted cockatoo.

Can you notice any differences in the feather condition of these cockatoos?

seem, for in so doing you are inviting disaster. Cockatoos may become jealous of the children in the household or any other person that they feel may threaten their relationship with their favorite person.

A jealous cockatoo can be a very dangerous bird toward those it does not like. If you want the bird to be a pet to both man and wife, you must arrange to spend your time with the bird equally. Even if you do, you may find that

The extraordinary-looking palm cockatoo has a long crest of hair-like feathers.

some birds still prefer one of you to the other. When acclimated properly, most cockatoos will direct their kind feelings toward both of you.

The intellectual capacity of cockatoos is astounding. They can understand simple and complex commands. They can speak words and sentences. They have excellent long-term and short-term memory. In a few days of consistent training they can become tame or learn a variety of tricks (depending, of course, on what you are doing as a trainer).

Some are capable of learning by watching another bird perform a trick (classic modeling behavior), while others must be taught to do the simplest tricks step by step.

A pair of Goffin's cockatoos. This Indonesian species has become more available for purchase because of the destruction of its natural habitat.

Long-billed corella. Note the length of its beak. This feature enables the bird to easily dig in the ground for sprouting seeds.

Cockatoos certainly do remember people, both those that they like and those that they dislike intensely. Even if a cockatoo has not seen you for years, it will often act toward you just as it did in the past. Some cockatoos insist upon having their life ordered in a certain way or they are unhappy. In other words, a liking for routine is one of the general traits of cockatoos. Interrupting long-standing routines can be the cause of emotional

disturbance or behavior problems
with your cockatoo.

The domestic-raised cockatoo is
not much different from the wild-
caught bird unless it is a hand-
reared baby. The personality of
the hand-reared bird is usually
affected by the foster relationship,
but this does not necessarily
mean that the bird will be more
affectionate, more gentle or easier
to train than an imported bird.

The average cockatoo is a

Above: A young yellow-tailed
cockatoo. **Facing page:** This photo
clearly illustrates the filamentous
feather crest of the gang-gang
cockatoo.

steady individual able to adjust
well to changes in environment.
Given a workable taming program,
the average bird progresses
quickly into a tame pet. Curious,
intelligent and highly emotional,
most cockatoos respond favorably

to gentle, consistent attention from a serious trainer.

There are cockatoos that are extremely nervous, anxiety-ridden individuals. The slightest movement of your hand will send these birds into a panic. They will jump from the training stand and run from you in any direction. Birds that constantly jump from the stand must be protected against injury by keeping them on low stands and adjusting your training techniques to include a very tranquil approach to taming. Given enough time and plenty of attention, the nervous cockatoo will become a socially well-adjusted member of your household. To be sure, the nervous bird is much more difficult to tame than most.

Even more difficult to socialize is the frantic cockatoo. These birds have little regard for their own safety in their attempts to run from you. They seem to refuse to accept their new surroundings and any sort of relationship with humans. These birds should be worked very low to the floor in a carefully prepared training area. It is imperative that you spend a great deal of time with these birds if you are serious about domesticating them. The behavior that I usually observe in frantic birds is a constant uncontrolled screaming whenever you approach. They refuse to maintain eye contact with you and run from your look!

Don't label your bird frantic to excuse yourself for not following through on a taming program. Frantic birds are rarely encountered. Give these birds at least five to six months of a sensible taming program with the focus on tranquility. These birds

Effective training requires much patience—and trust—on your part.

When introducing cockatoos of different species, or even birds of the same species, it is always wise to observe their reactions to one another before leaving them alone together.

must have a well-ordered daily routine to give them as much stability as possible. (At least they will know what to expect as far as feeding and cleaning times). If you

Above: Cockatoos are alert, inquisitive creatures. *Facing page:* A male galah. The eye ring of the male of this species is more pronounced than that of the female of this species.

can't deal with the bird at all, give it to someone with more experience or a better environment. You may be able to work out a trade for a more suitable bird with someone in the bird business. (A hobbyist, breeder or professional trainer may be interested in attempting to help the bird adjust). But keep in mind that the most effective way to change the bird's behavior is to

Simple daily routines such as feeding will enhance the bond between your pet and you.

The sulphur-crested cockatoo is one of the more commonly kept species of cockatoo.

put in the time necessary to achieve the task. Don't cheat on the taming time and blame the bird for your inconsistency.

Your wild cockatoo may be very aggressive and strike out at you viciously. This is not often the case, but you may encounter an aggressive biting bird. Usually you can modify the biting behavior and eventually extinguish it completely. This requires careful observation of the cockatoo's

behavior in all that it does. You can avoid being hurt by paying attention to what you are doing whenever dealing with the bird. You may mistake the fear bite for an act of hostility and react

An occasional peck at your finger during a training session is not cause for alarm, but a consistently aggressive pet may require a behavior modification program.

improperly. The way in which you react to bird-biting can help solve the problem or make it much worse. Begin taming with the use of a behavior modification program to help you in designing an effective approach to taming an aggressive cockatoo. Do not begin by striking back at it.

Some people refer to very frantic or aggressive biting birds as "broncos." This is usually not the case, but when a person cannot understand and effectively deal with a difficult cockatoo he may justify it by labeling the bird a bronco. This is not to suggest that every cockatoo has the same pet potential, for some will become satisfying pets, while others may resist all of your sincere efforts to tame them. When a trainer tells you that he has run into a number of bronco cockatoos, he has not mastered the skill of taming. By all means look for another qualified trainer to assist you in taming the bird, but never let it be abused, starved or tranquilized, no matter how much confidence you may have in the trainer. A humane training program achieves the best results. Deprivation or startle techniques should not be used. You probably will never run into a bronco, but if after five to eight months of consistent, sensible taming you don't get positive progress, you may be able to trade the bird to a breeder. Breeders are more interested in how the bird relates to other birds

In captivity and when tamed, the palm cockatoo has the reputation of being a very gentle bird.

than in how it relates to people.

Do not sell such a bird to an unsuspecting private individual without telling the person of the behavior problems that you have encountered. Try to find the best possible situation for a cockatoo that you feel is untrainable. Talk to zoos with bird collections and you may find it an excellent home. Examine all reasonable alternatives before condemning the difficult cockatoo to a life of

When fed and housed properly, cockatoos are generally hardy birds.

confinement in a small cage.

Many cockatoos are moody and, like some people, swing from elation to depression. Some can be considered emotionally disturbed. This may seem impossible for a bird, but cockatoos are not your average chicken! Their emotional complexity is similar to that of humans. I have seen cockatoos have nervous breakdowns after being separated from a well-loved former owner. Some birds that have lived for many years as single pets in a private cage do not adjust well to life in a flight cage with other cockatoos. They are often intimidated by the other birds and do not compete for food if it is served community-style. They often relate better to the human attending to the maintenance of the cage than to the other birds. These birds may develop self-destructive behavior if an attempt is not made to help them adjust.

In conclusion, the newly acquired cockatoo is an individual with a definite personality. The great majority are natural hams and react quickly to your attempts to tame them. They are inquisitive and appreciate a well-ordered lifestyle. Most thrive for many years in a suitable environment. The maladjusted, aggressive, frantic cockatoos are few and far between. They have been mentioned here to help you understand the idiosyncracies of owning a cockatoo. Do not try to fit your bird into one of these personality types, for it takes months before the true personality of your new pet emerges. All of the information on personality is here to assist you, the inexperienced owner of a wild cockatoo, in appreciating the bird's complex emotional makeup. The information will also help you greatly in developing an effective approach to taming the cockatoo.

Most cockatoos are intelligent, adaptable creatures.

Choosing a Healthy Cockatoo

When you are going to buy a cockatoo, it should satisfy the following criteria for good health. The eyes must be clear and alert. There should be no lumps, bumps or scratches on the eye ring. There should be no evidence of discharge from the eyes. The nares (nasal openings) must be clean and open. There should be no dirt or discharge on or around the nares. Both nasal openings should be round and regularly shaped. They should not extend down into the beak matter. There should be no sign of red irritation around the nasal openings.

The beak should fit together evenly with the upper mandible neatly closing over the lower. There should be no signs of extensive wear on either mandible. Spots of white or yellow on the beak matter may indicate a fungus or injury to the beak. The upper mandible should be of a proper length, not overgrown.

The feet should be in perfect condition, with four toes on each foot, two in the front and two in the rear. Each toe should have a claw. One missing toe or claw is not a serious disability, but two or more missing toes can be a problem. The bird should have equal gripping strength in both feet. If the bird appears to favor one foot, think twice before buying it. There should be even heat in both feet. If you can get the opportunity to feel the feet of the cockatoo, check to see that there is equal heat in both feet. One warm foot and one cold foot can indicate a problem.

The wings should ideally be fully feathered. There should be no evidence of lumps or bumps at the base of the wing feathers. If the bird has a wing clipped, check to see that it was done correctly. Only one wing should be clipped. Neither wing should droop. Both wings should be held snugly to the body. Birds that hold their wings out from the body are usually overheated.

The overall plumage should be smooth. No bare patches of skin should show through the feathering. A few broken tail feathers are nothing to worry about, but if the tail appears to be chewed off, the bird may have done the chewing itself. Be careful not to buy a feather chewer.

The legs should be of equal thickness, and the scales of the legs smooth. There should be no obvious bumps, cuts or sores on the legs. There should be no yellow or white spots either.

The vent must be clean, free of any soiling. It should not be distended.

Observe the bird's droppings, for they are the best indicators of health. The droppings should have form, and both white and dark green matter. Kelly green, brown,

Facing page: A pair of palm cockatoos. Notice the smoothness of the overall plumage of these birds.

black, yellow or orange droppings may indicate a digestive disorder. Droppings that are mostly water also indicate ill health.

Whenever possible, have the seller hold the bird so that you can feel the amount of meat on the breast. A thin bird should never be purchased, no matter how gentle it appears. Thin birds usually have a

medical problem.

In summation, the eyes should be clear, bright and alert. The nares, free of discharge and dirt, should be regularly shaped and

As well as having a striking appearance, cockatoos are active, interesting birds.

This sulphur-crested demonstrates the potential that some cockatoos have for learning complex tricks.

not extend into the beak matter. The beak should fit evenly together, the upper mandible fitting over the lower. No discoloration should appear on either mandible. The feet, legs and toes should have even heat and equal gripping strength. The scales should be smooth and have no yellow or white spots. The claws should not be overgrown. The plumage should be smooth with no bare skin visible. Feathers of the tail and wings should have a minimum of breakage or you

may be buying a feather chewer. The vent must be free of soiling and the droppings should have solid form, with both dark green and white matter. The bird must not be thin when you feel the breast. There should be no lumps, bumps or sores anywhere on the bird's body.

Step back and observe the bird's respiration. Breathing should be slow and even, not rapid, irregular or labored. The bird should have good posture and not sit low to the perch.

IMPERFECT BIRDS

Some sellers may offer a cockatoo at a reduced price if it has a handicap such as a bad eye, a drooped wing or a crooked leg. These handicapped birds may become good pets if proper care

is given, but never buy an imperfect bird for a high price. If the bird has chewed off most of its feathers, the seller may again lower the price. It is not advisable to purchase a bird with very poor plumage, for in most cases feather-chewing behavior is very difficult to modify.

If you do purchase an imperfect cockatoo, go to the veterinarian and have the bird checked out completely. Chances are that the handicaps may be worse than you think. On the other hand, the vet may tell you that it is a minor disability and not to worry. Remember not to pay a premium price for an imperfect cockatoo.

WHERE TO BUY A COCKATOO

Your local pet shop is the most logical—and in most cases certainly the most accessible—source of supply when you're in the market to buy a cockatoo. Although not every pet shop keeps cockatoos in stock at all times, even those that don't are in a much better position than you are to obtain a bird. Therefore, unless you have contact with a reliable source of supply other than a pet shop (a breeder perhaps), you'll probably be better off by starting your search among pet shops in your area. Pet shops, because they stay put and depend

Preening is an essential task to a cockatoo.

Even the hardest seed hulls are no match for the mighty beak of the palm cockatoo.

Left: The yellow-tailed cockatoo is a beautiful bird, but it is rarely found outside its natural habitat, Australia. Facing page: A Major Mitchell's, or Leadbeater's, cockatoo (Cacatua leadbeateri). The genus is represented by species with very well-developed and erectile crests.

on the good will of the populace within their area, can be much more reliable than some other sources of supply—some of which are here today and gone tomorrow.

You may be fortunate enough to locate a breeder of cockatoos. A hobbyist who has had luck will usually have marvelous cockatoo babies for sale, but they will be much more expensive than the imported birds. In short, the responsible, reliable retailer may be your best source for buying a cockatoo, especially if you are not familiar with cockatoos and cannot readily identify a healthy bird when you see it.

Never buy a cockatoo on impulse. Examine all of the possible sources and spend some time looking before you buy. When you find the right bird, a healthy, attractive individual, one that appears to be steady at the right price, by all means buy it.

Incidentally, here is a simple test by which you can determine whether the bird offered to you is tame. A tame bird should:
1. Step on and off your arm without panic.
2. Refrain from biting.
3. Not flutter away when you touch the feathers.

Remember that the fearless bird is consistently the most gentle.

Environment

Most people buy a cockatoo and keep it indoors as a house pet. The proper environment for the caged house pet includes both an adequate cage and a sturdy bird stand. The cage should be large enough for the bird to flap its wings without touching the sides. It is not recommended that you restrict the cockatoo to a stand 24 hours a day. The stand does not give the bird enough security at night if it should be frightened by a household noise. In addition, it does not give the bird room to climb around.

The best room in which to keep your cockatoo is the family room where you spend most of your recreational time. Keep the bird away from air conditioning vents or dry radiator heat. Cold temperatures do not harm a healthy bird, but drafts do. Dry heat can cause dehydration. Keep the bird away from the kitchen, where temperatures may fluctuate during cooking times. The cage and stand should be kept away from the doors and windows if you live in a cold climate. If your bird is flighted, be certain to keep it away from doors at all times.

If you have a screened patio, with shelter from the elements, you may consider keeping the cockatoo outside for most of the year. If it gets very cold outside, below 40°F, it is best to bring the bird inside until it warms up. If heavy rain blows onto the patio, you should bring the bird in until

weather improves.

You may keep your cockatoo in an outdoor flight cage. The outdoor aviary must be made rodent-proof and have adequate shelter for the bird to roost or get out of the rain. Shade the outdoor aviary from direct sunlight or you may end up cooking your bird.

The outdoor aviary must be easy to clean and ideally has a double door to prevent accidental escape as you enter or exit. The floor should be easy to clean and disinfect. The door should be kept locked to prevent the bird from opening the latch and escaping.

Some people like to give their birds a light shower. The cockatoos usually enjoy the gentle spray of a shower, but be cautious. Going from the high temperature and humidity in the shower to the cooler temperature in the other rooms of your home can bring on illness. Allow the bird time to dry and repowder itself.

Other environments in which a cockatoo may thrive are wildlife parks and zoos with adequate facilities for parrots. You may want to keep your bird as a free-flying pet, but this should not be considered if you live in a residential community. For those fortunate people that live out in the country, keeping the cockatoo at liberty is a possibility, but one in

Facing page: Cockatoos have short tails, compared to their body length.

which caution must be exercised. Remember to train your bird very well before releasing it to fly out on its own if you expect it to return in the afternoon for feeding and roosting. There is a great deal to consider before allowing your bird to fly freely outdoors.

Your cockatoo may fall prey to children with BB pistols, or to large domesticated cats and dogs. Birds native to the area are not often a threat to the free-flying cockatoo unless they are large birds of prey.

Cockatoos are not recommended as store birds. They are far too moody to be considered safe with the majority of patrons in your store.

DIETARY REQUIREMENTS

When you bring the new cockatoo home, have the cage prepared with fresh water and feed before placing it inside. The feed should include sunflower seed, a few raw peanuts, a slice of banana, a slice of apple, an orange section and a piece of raw corn. Sprinkle the fruit and vegetables with a vitamin-mineral supplement. Use it sparingly or the bird may refuse to accept food with the supplement on it.

Often a newly acquired cockatoo will refuse to eat on the first day that you get it, since it feels insecure in the new environment. If the bird does not eat for twenty-four hours, do not panic. The bird should accept at least sunflower seed on the

second day. If your bird has refused all feed for 48 hours, be certain to phone the seller and inquire as to the bird's former diet.

Most healthy cockatoos will accept sunflower seed, raw corn, peanuts and a variety of other fruits and vegetables in a very short time. Remember that you must teach the bird to eat properly, just as you have to teach a child. Many months may pass before the cockatoo is eating a well-balanced diet, but always provide the suggested foods even if the bird refuses them at first. To avoid waste, do not offer large portions of fruit. In general, provide the bird with a variety of different foods.

A good daily feeding program includes a measured amount of sunflower seed, a few raw peanuts, one green and one yellow vegetable (raw), and two fruits. Some people feel that it is incorrect to feed citrus fruit to parrots. I have never discovered any basis for thinking that citrus fruit is detrimental to cockatoos. I have found that most cockatoos greatly enjoy squeezing out the juice of an orange or grapefruit slice. Be moderate, however, in the amount of citrus fruit that you provide the cockatoo.

Do not feed lots of soft food and a small amount of seed or you may find that your bird has watery stools. Feed a well-balanced ration of seed and fruit and vegetables every day.

A red-tailed cockatoo. The red band on the tail feathers is present only in the male.

Vitamin supplements are recommended to sprinkle on the soft foods, water, and oil is recommended for the seed. If you prefer to mix cod liver oil and wheat germ oil in equal portions, go ahead and use it. Do not overuse oil supplements. Corn oil is not recommended. Do not use regular cooking oils.

Some newly acquired cockatoos may absolutely refuse to eat seed with oil on it. In this case, be certain to put only two or three drops of oil on the seed on alternating days. It is best to introduce supplements into the diet gradually. Do not use a high concentration of vitamin supplements at first, but do be sure to add it to the fresh water every day. Always introduce it gradually.

Do not deprive the bird of feed in your first attempts to tame it. You cannot tame a sick bird. Your first consideration must be to get

new cockatoo eating a well-balanced diet.

Young baby birds or old or sick cockatoos may require two or more feedings per day. If you find yourself always refilling the bird dish, and if it seems that the bird is losing weight, be certain to see a bird veterinarian immediately. Your bird may be showing symptoms of illness if it eats a great deal and loses weight.

Very young birds or very old ones may need more feed to maintain their body weight than other cockatoos. Be certain to feed all birds an adequate amount of feed.

You may provide an aviary-size mineral block for the bird to chew.

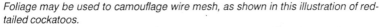

Foliage may be used to camouflage wire mesh, as shown in this illustration of red-tailed cockatoos.

This is desirable if the cockatoo does not chew it to powder within five minutes. It is waste of a mineral block if the bird crumbles it to nothing. If your bird nibbles at the mineral block and does not destroy it, do be certain to provide one at all times.

Most cockatoos do not seem to eat the gravel mixtures that are commonly marketed for smaller birds. If you live near a farm supply, you may purchase pigeon-size gravel mixture. Buy crushed granite grit and crushed oyster shells, and combine them into one mixture. Put the gravel into a clean dish instead of on the cage bottom. Watch to see whether the cockatoo eats the gravel or not. Either way, go ahead and provide the gravel and be sure to replace old gravel with new when needed or at least once a month.

In flight, galahs constantly make piercing contact calls to keep the flock together.

Taming

TAMING THE WILD COCKATOO

Although taming a wild bird can be accomplished with a fully flighted bird, the clipping of flight feathers on one wing is recommended for most people that plan to keep and tame the bird inside their homes. Clipping the feathers should be done only by an experienced bird handler or veterinarian who is familiar with the procedure. Many veterinarians are not experienced bird handlers and may not clip the feathers in the most desirable manner.

Clipping the feathers to prevent flight must not be so extensive that the bird is subject to injury from falling. To clip the wing, first gather the necessary tools and think about what you are going to

do before beginning. Then be as fast and careful as possible.

You should have a steady person assist you with the manicure of both flight feathers and claws. The holder must be calm enough to hold the bird properly, neither injuring it nor getting one of you bitten. The first step is capturing the bird. Using a good-sized towel, reach into the cage and place it over the bird's head. Calmly catch the bird behind the head and neck, being certain not to exert too much force

Below: This cockatoo has been taught to "play dead." ***Facing page:*** *The cockatoo's claws are excellent gripping tools.*

Left: The mesh in a net used to capture a bird must be small enough to prevent the bird from becoming entangled if it thrashes around. *Below:* Wing clipping is basically a two-person operation. *Facing page:* Blood feathers, new feathers that are still being nourished by a blood vessel while they grow, must not be cut.

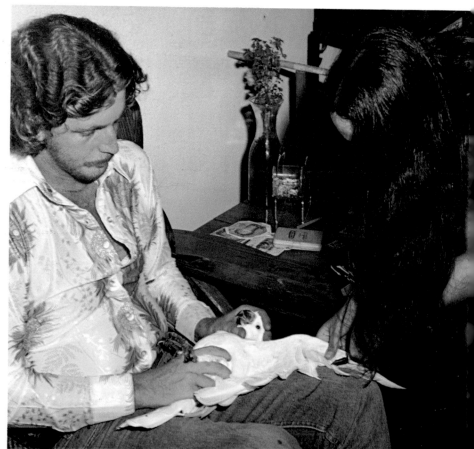

or allow the head to twist around dangerously. Remember that if you grab the bird incorrectly you may break its neck or be bitten severely. Once you have control of the bird's head, reach down and catch the feet. A second person can be of great assistance if you need help. Have the other person grab the feet and hold them out gently as you take hold, placing two fingers between the legs to secure the bird.

Now turn the bird over on its back and hold it gently but firmly against your towel-covered lap or a well-padded counter top. Never restrain a cockatoo on a hard surface or hold it out in the air when clipping feather or claws. By so doing you invite disaster. It is your responsibility to hold the bird securely and safely, keep a watch on its respiration, and tell the person doing the clipping if you are losing control of the bird. Never let go of a bird without giving proper warning.

When you are treating a bird that is injured or very frightened, be sure to watch the eyes and respiration to avoid putting the bird into shock. Two steady people working together can usually accomplish the manicure without much difficulty and in a relatively short time.

An alternative to towel capture (often best for beginners wary of flapping wings) is the bird net. When capturing a cockatoo in a net, lower it over the bird's head.

Carefully use one hand to grasp the bird gently and securely behind the head and neck. Cockatoos have long skinny necks and can be difficult to hold without the head twisting. The second person should free the bird's feet of the net. Then, while you hold the feet with one hand and retain your gentle grip on the head and neck with the other, allow your assistant to disengage the net, being careful not to snag the beak. Try to hold the bird's head and cradle the neck with your fingers. Do not push the head into the shoulders or pull it. Don't let it twist. Try not to rub against the eyes; do not destroy the crest feathers.

You need good light for manicuring. Gather your tools: a sharp pair of cloth scissors, a small wire cutter, and a styptic powder. For clipping claws you may use a wire-cutter or a guillotine-style clipper. Also have an emery board or metal nail file to smooth rough edges.

To clip the wing, first look at both wings and decide which one to clip. Ideally both wings will have no new feathers growing in. New feathers are called blood feathers, for they are nourished by a blood vessel that runs through the center of the feather. Once the feather is grown, the vessel seals off at the follicle and no longer transmits blood into the quill. Always be certain that you can identify blood feathers before

In contrast to his solemn look and somber color, the yellow-tailed cockatoo makes a very engaging pet.

clipping. If you cannot, do not attempt the clipping. If both wings are free of blood feathers, leave the better feathered wing alone and clip the other. Leave the two end primaries as they are. Cut the next feather in half with the scissors. Now push back the small under feather coverts to expose the quill of each feather. Use the wire-clipper to clip the feather straight across the quill, leaving at least two inches of feather quill sticking out of the wing to prevent

damage to the wing. If you have a blood feather between two grown feathers, tip it and clip the feathers on either side of it the same length to prevent breakage.

Many cockatoos can fly well with an improperly clipped or under-clipped wing. They are strong flyers and lightweight birds. Once you know your pet's flying habits you can alter the number of clipped feathers, but at first a fairly heavy clip is recommended. A heavy clip means that you leave

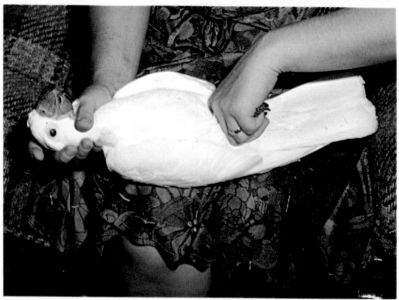

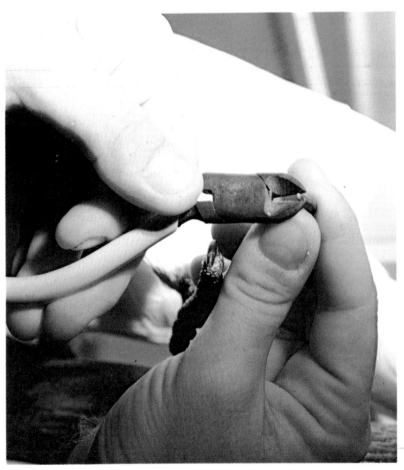

Facing page: It is not wise to hold the bird out in the air during the process of clipping claws or wings. Instead, the bird should be cradled gently but firmly in the lap, with head and feet securely held. *Above:* In clipping the claws, remove only the tip of the claw. Work cautiously, being very careful not to cut into the vein.

just three or four feathers next to the bird's torso, clipping off at least ten or 12 feathers. Always be certain to leave the first three feathers on the end of the wing unclipped. This will help cushion the end of the wing if the bird takes a fall.

Keep a close watch to see how often the clipped feathers fall out and replace themselves, especially if you take the bird outside with you. People who think their bird is grounded can be amazed to see their cockatoo fly off into a tall tree, or sometimes out of sight! Make it a regular practice to check the wing each time you go out with the bird.

Some people feel that clipping the wing is cruel and does not allow the bird enough liberty. These same people will use a leg chain to keep their pets in tow. I feel that clipping periodically is much preferred to the use of a leg chain. Cockatoos get plenty of exercise in a well ordered environment without flying, but may meet a sad demise if they escape out the door to unfamiliar and often unfriendly surroundings. In addition, leg chains may harm the bird if it jumps away in fear or falls from the perch. I never recommend a leg chain for any cockatoo (or any other parrot for that matter).

To clip the claws, use the clippers to tip off the end of each claw. Just take a bit at a time, for if you take too much you may hit a vein. If you do hit blood, stop the manicure and press styptic powder into the bleeding tip. Hold a moment and the bleeding should stop. Do not file nails that bleed when you clip them. If bleeding stops in a moment, finish the manicure by filing each claw. If bleeding is heavy and difficult to stop, forget the manicure and just be certain to stop the bleeding. You may have to take the claw and dip it into the powder or use a dry cotton swab to press against the styptic powder. When bleeding stops, place the bird carefully into its cage and leave it alone to calm down. If a bird is nervous, its heart beats faster and bleeding continues.

To release the bird after clipping it, you should place it onto the floor; release the feet first and then the head. Never drop the cockatoo to the floor. If it is a wild bird, it will probably fall off a stand. Once the wing is clipped, let the bird settle down for a minute and then begin training it. There is no need to clip the bird and then to begin taming at a later date. Wing clipping is considered a preliminary to taming the bird.

In the prepared taming area begin your first lesson. The best taming area is a small room with ample padding on the floor and few obstacles for the bird to climb under or bang into. Wear proper clothing when taming your bird. Heavy garments are not recommended. Gloves are not considered tools for taming. Your clothing should not be made of materials that snag easily and catch the bird's claws. You are asking to be bitten by grabbing the bird or letting it get caught on your clothing, jewelry, or hair.

The taming area must have a low bird stand, stable enough to hold the bird without tipping over. Get some dowels or natural wood training sticks. You'll need two short (12-inch) dowels at least 1½ inches in diameter and one or two long ones (2 feet) of the same diameter. A net is not a taming or training tool and should not be used to retrieve the bird during a lesson. Netting the bird is not going to help tame it and should only be done when quick capture is imperative.

THE FIRST LESSONS

The first time that you release the cockatoo into the taming area, be prepared to spend the entire lesson teaching the bird to step on and off the training stick. Some smart birds accomplish this primary behavior in the first lesson. Others may take many patient hours of work to learn to perch on the training stick without jumping. Place the stick in front of the bird's breast and coax it to step on. These first lessons should be conducted with the bird on the padded floor. Your back may suffer at first, but if you work seriously the cockatoo will soon be sitting on a bird stand.

If the bird pushes the stick away or refuses to step up, a gentle touch of the stick may cause it to move its feet. Don't badger a frightened cockatoo. Be willing to spend many hours just talking to the bird about these basic behaviors.

While drilling the bird in stepping on and off the stick, keep

A wooden toy ladder makes a comfortable perch for this cockatoo.

Left: The first lessons in teaching your pet to step onto and off the training stick should be performed in an area having a padded floor. *Below:* Training the bird to perch on the training stick is preparation for having it perch on its stand. *Facing page:* Be sure that the training stick is of adequate thickness.

it low to the floor to protect the bird from injury. Some cockatoos step onto the stick immediately. With these birds, wait a few moments before setting them back on the floor. If the bird tries to climb up the stick and onto your arm, discourage it at first by holding the stick perpendicular to your body and your elbow bent naturally.

Give the bird a couple of lessons with the stick before letting it climb up to your shoulder. This is suggested to prevent any possible injury to both trainer and bird. If you go slowly and acclimate your bird, it may never bite you during the taming process. I believe that the cockatoo experiences great surges of emotion before it bites you. Of course, most people react to being bitten by dropping the creature or hitting it to make it stop. Such mishaps are not inevitable if you work steadily, consistently and seriously with a wild-caught cockatoo. The great majority of cockatoos are docile but emotional creatures and bite mostly from anxiety, not aggression. If you do not excite and frighten the bird, you probably won't get bitten.

Some cockatoos can be very difficult to stick-train. Some stubbornly refuse to step onto the stick, while others run to a corner of the training area and scream at you. You may spend many hours in the first lessons just stick-training the bird. If you put in the time, you will achieve the desired goal. You must give the cockatoo a lesson several times a day if necessary. Daily lessons are the key to taming wild cockatoos. Two days of lessons followed by two days of no handling will not tame the bird.

Once you have accomplished stick-training, teach the bird to sit on a bird stand. Drill it in stepping from the stick to the stand and back again. When the cockatoo is at ease stepping from the stick to the stand, substitute your arm for the stick, and drill the bird in the same manner. Use one hand to distract the cockatoo and offer your arm to the bird. If the bird tries to bite you, do not strike it. Move your free hand to distract it from your arm. Deliver a loud "no." If the bird tries to bite constantly, do more drill work with the stick before offering your arm again.

Many cockatoos that I have tamed allowed petting before they would step onto my arm. You may try this approach, but always watch the bird and move slowly and deliberately. Under no circumstances strike the bird. This will accomplish nothing. Striking the bird may intimidate it, but it will never help to strengthen its confidence in you as a friend.

The best results in taming are achieved when the lessons are conducted many times every day for short periods of time. Once the bird has learned to step on and off your arm, a stick and the stand, you may begin moving around the house with the bird. Move very slowly and do not venture far from the taming area at first, in case the bird gets nervous and jumps to the floor. If so, retrieve the bird with your hand or a stick. Go back to the taming area and begin again.

Most cockatoos enjoy being petted and will allow you to stroke the crest feathers and touch the wings or tail. Each day try to touch the bird a little more. Do not force yourself on the bird. Work slowly and consistently to achieve the desired goal.

TAMING A COCKATOO THAT WAS SOMEONE ELSE'S PET

You may buy your cockatoo from a person who can no longer keep it. If the bird was living with the person for a year or more, you may find that the bird is slow to accept handling by a new owner, especially one of the opposite sex from the former owner.

Take your time in making friends with this type of bird. Again, do not strike the bird for biting you. Teach it to accept feed from your hand and talk to the bird. You may not have to go through the formalities of basic taming, but you have to devote many hours before the bird accepts you.

In time, with patience and consistent handling, the bird should come around. Structure the

An adult male white cockatoo displaying his crest, which looks like an upside-down umbrella.

bird's daily activities, for routine will help it to adjust to a new environment. Feed and clean the cage at the same time each day. Use the same words in each lesson to develop a verbal rapport with the bird.

Above: *This cockatoo is being trained to display one wing in a gesture of greeting, and it has already mastered the elements of the trick.* ***Facing page:*** *No matter how well trained a cockatoo is or how well it has adapted to living as a household pet, under certain conditions (being badly frightened, for example) it will forget what it has learned and will react instinctively, possibly even striking out at its owner/trainer.*

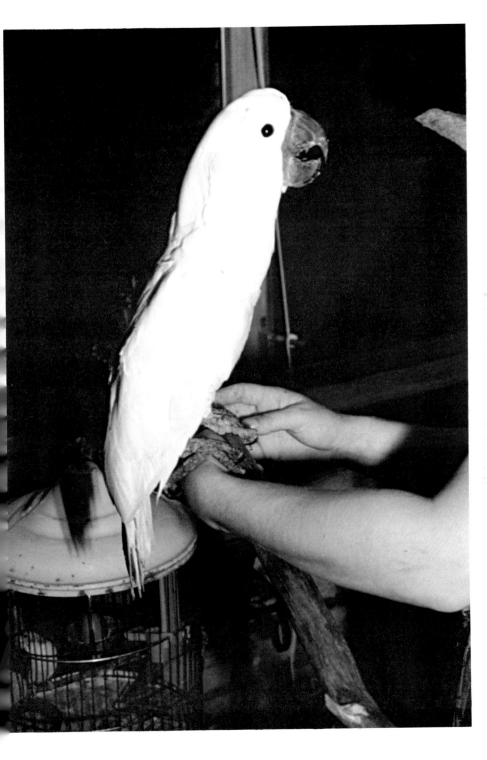

Special Behavior Problems

Some cockatoos have particular behavior problems. The most common are screaming for attention and extreme jealousy of one or more family members. Unprovoked biting and destruction of household furnishings can result.

Modifying such behavior usually takes a long period of time, a sensible behavior program and an enthusiastic trainer. A behavior modification program must be considered carefully, for if administered incorrectly it may actually reinforce the unwanted behavior.

The cockatoo that screams for attention is probably the most difficult to modify. Screaming is natural for most parrots. Do not attempt to pacify the bird every time it yelps. Although you may get the bird to be quiet by giving it food or a toy, you are not teaching the bird to be quiet. On the contrary, you are rewarding the bird for screaming if you appease it.

Carefully observe the time and situation in which the bird screams most often. Sometimes you can eliminate screaming by ignoring the bird completely or covering the cage until the bird gets quiet. Once it is quiet for three minutes (don't wait too long), remove the cover. Now is the time to pay attention to the bird. In other words, attend to the bird for not screaming. This type of behavior program is not easy to administer. Covering the cage may not work. Some birds will pull the cover off in one minute and commence yelling. Give careful thought to the behavior before attempting to change it. Remember that cockatoos are naturally noisy birds

This perky little character is a white cockatoo.

Facing page: *A salmon-crested cockatoo.*

Left: Petting—or any other physical contact with your bird—should always be done calmly and gently. **Below:** This bird has learned the trick of displaying his wing. **Facing page:** Cockatoos' claws and beaks can be wielded destructively. People (especially children) who cannot be expected to act sensibly around a cockatoo should be prevented from having any contact with it.

and it is very difficult to remove an inherent trait. If you can't live with some noise at sunset, do not get a cockatoo.

Jealousy of people that a bird perceives as threatening to its relationship with its owner may result in unprovoked biting. Be aware of this and do not take chances with your friends or children. If the bird attaches itself to one person, it is not uncommon for it to resent other people. In most cases you can modify this bad behavior if you allow other family members to attend to the bird's feed, water, cage maintenance and, hopefully, some handling of the bird without you (the favorite person) present.

After your pet is accustomed to being handled, you can teach it to step onto your hand.

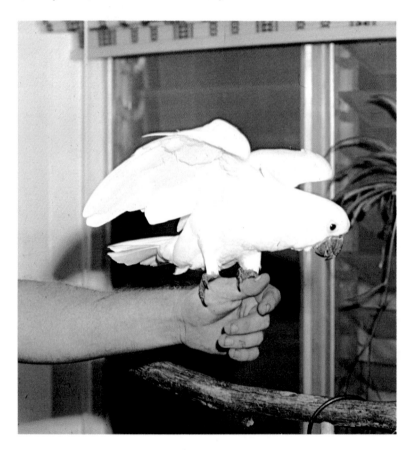

Never allow children to handle a cockatoo without your supervision. Keep the kids and the bird apart if necessary to protect them both. This is not to suggest that most cockatoos will attack your friends and children, for some birds will allow anyone to pet them. For the hard core jealous cockatoos, be realistic. Changing the behavior is possible if all parties involved participate over a long period of time.

Destruction of furniture or curtains can be eliminated if you give the bird an outlet for its natural tendency to chew. Cockatoos are notorious chewers. Always provide the bird with adequate chewing material. Fresh branches and pieces of two by one inch lumber will help channel the cockatoo's natural desire to chew. Do not expect to eliminate chewing behavior, for it is an innate trait of most cockatoos. Do channel the behavior by providing chewing material on a daily basis.

Female galah.

Facing page: Once a rapport has been established between bird and owner, the cockatoo will gladly accept tidbits fed by hand and will react favorably when stroked or petted. ***Above:*** It makes sense to regularly examine your pet for any signs of illness or disease.

Advanced Training

Once you have taught the cockatoo the basics of social behavior, you may consider advanced training. To repeat, the basics of social behavior include (1) having the bird step onto your arm and remain there without biting, (2) having the bird sit on the outside stand for extended periods of time, and (3) stick training. Advanced training cannot be accomplished until the basics have been successfully mastered by the new cockatoo.

To teach the bird to remain at liberty, as a free flyer, is not easy to achieve. If you live in an urban or residential area, do not even consider teaching your cockatoo to fly freely outdoors. A screened patio may seem safe to you, but most cockatoos can chew their way through screening in a few minutes, escaping to the outdoors. For people that live in the country, far away from city noises and traffic, liberty may be considered. It is imperative that the bird first learn to know the boundaries of your property while its wings are clipped. You may think that a leg chain is more humane than clipping the flight feathers, but I do not think so. Leg chains are not recommended under any circumstances if you plan to follow the taming and training regimen outlined in this book.

Every day take the clipped bird outside and place it on the bird stand with water. Always supervise your pet, even if it is not aware of your presence. At the same time each day take the bird back into the house and feed it immediately. Do not place food on the outside stand. Always feed the bird as soon as you return it to the house. As the flight feathers grow back, you may find that it is

Left: A pair of gang-gang cockatoos, the male quite conspicuous with its scarlet head. *Facing page:* Note the healthy condition of this bird's feathers.

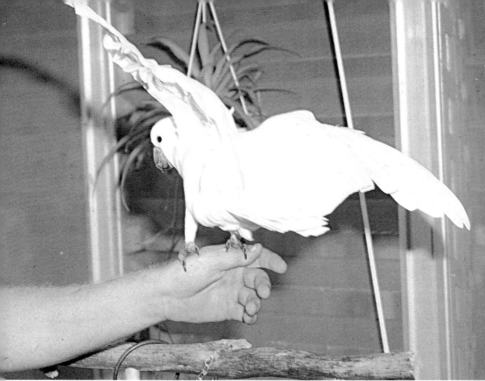

Facing page, top: Displaying the wings is one of the tricks that most cockatoos are able to learn. *Facing page, bottom:* The wing-clipped bird can be taught to bob its head while displaying the wings. *Above:* Your pet may have a tendency toward unsteadiness at first after it has learned to spread its wings in response to your cue.

necessary to clip them again. Some birds may fly away to a tall tree and refuse to come down until they are thirsty and hungry. Do not try to acclimate your cockatoo to liberty-training quickly. This training may take a year to accomplish. Always retrieve the bird in the afternoon no matter how warm the weather. Otherwise you cannot keep a careful watch on the bird's health and food intake.

Remember, teaching the bird to remain at liberty is not recommended unless you live in a quiet, secluded area with enough acreage to keep the bird on your property at all times.

SPEECH AND TRICK TRAINING

Speech training can be accomplished by a motivated trainer if lessons are given daily and the material is not altered until the bird has mastered it. Begin with simple one-syllable or two-syllable words and conduct your lessons in a quiet room devoid of outside interference. Lessons can be given for five minutes several times a day. This is much preferred to a 30 minute lesson once a day. Tape recorded lessons are not recommended. If a bird learns to speak with no persons present, he may not speak when they are.

Tricks should also be taught in short lessons several times a day. Do not expect your bird to learn complicated tricks in a short period of time. If you cannot follow through on trick training, it is better not to attempt it. Very simple tricks that most cockatoos can learn without too much difficulty are displaying the wings, bobbing the head and placing objects into a container.

Watch your bird and observe it at play. Try to capitalize on its natural antics. Reinforce its natural behavior to teach it tricks on a command basis.

The advanced training of cockatoos is a very complicated subject and would require a separate volume to discuss fully. The purpose of this book is primarily to help individuals tame and socialize their pet cockatoos, for most people have a difficult time teaching basic taming to a bird.

Index

Overleaf: Cockatoos are intelligent animals capable of learning what you want them to do if you approach the task with patience.

TAMING AND TRAINING COCKATOOS
KW-071